DOLLEY Madison

SPIRIT
of America®

DOLLEY *Madison*

FIRST LADY

By Cynthia Klingel and Robert B. Noyed

The
Child's
World

The Child's World®
Chanhassen, Minnesota

7

DOLLEY *Madison*

Published in the United States of America by The Child's World®
PO Box 326 • Chanhassen, MN 55317-0326 • 800-599-READ • www.childsworld.com

Acknowledgments

The Child's World®: Mary Berendes, Publishing Director

Editorial Directions, Inc.: E. Russell Primm, Emily Dolbear, and Lucia Raatma, Editors; Linda S. Koutris, Photo Selector; Dawn Friedman, Photo Research; Red Line Editorial, Fact Research; Irene Keller, Copy Editor; Tim Griffin/IndexServ, Indexer; Chad Rubel, Proofreader

Photo

Cover: North Wind Picture Archives; Bettmann/Corbis: 6, 12, 13; Lee Snider/Corbis: 9; Carl and Ann Purcell/Corbis: 17; Hulton Archive/Getty Images: 15; Michael Evans/Newsmakers/Getty Images: 21; Greensboro Historical Museum Archives: 27; Library of Congress: 10, 25; The Library of Virginia: 7 top; North Wind Picture Archives: 2, 7 bottom, 11, 18, 19 bottom, 22, 28; Stock Montage: 14, 23, 26; The White House Collection, courtesy of the White House Historical Association: 16 (#123), 19 top (#55), 20 (#661), 24 (#21).

Registration

Library of Congress Cataloging-in-Publication Data
Klingel, Cynthia Fitterer.
  Dolley Madison : first lady / by Cynthia Klingel and Robert B. Noyed.
    p. cm.
  Includes index.
  Summary: Briefly describes the life of First Lady Dolley Madison, including her accomplishments and her impact on American history.
  ISBN 1-56766-170-X (Library Bound : alk. paper)
  1. Madison, Dolley, 1768–1849—Juvenile literature. 2. Presidents' spouses—United States—Biography—Juvenile literature. [1. Madison, Dolley, 1768–1849. 2. First ladies. 3. Women—Biography.] I. Noyed, Robert B. II. Title.
  E342.1 .K575 2003
  973.5'1'092—dc21

2001007402

12   23   27

Contents

Chapter ONE

A Quaker Girl

A portrait of Dolley Madison in later life

DOLLEY MADISON WAS ONE OF THE best-known first ladies in the United States. She was married to James Madison, the fourth president of the United States. Some have called Dolley Madison the country's first first lady. Dolley Payne was born on May 20, 1768, near what is now Guilford County in North Carolina. Dolley's parents were John and Mary Coles Payne. When Dolley was an infant, her family moved to a farm in Virginia called Scotchtown. The

Payne family lived in Scotchtown for about 14 years.

Dolley's parents were **Quakers**. The Quakers believed in a simple way of life. Dolley was not allowed to dance or sing. She wore gray dresses and plain **bonnets**. But she was a happy child.

At that time, most people believed that only boys should go to school. But Quakers thought that girls should also go to school. Dolley was allowed to attend school and she was very smart. She was also beautiful.

In 1783, Dolley's father sold the farm and freed the family's slaves. The family then moved to Philadelphia in

Scotchtown, in Hanover County, Virginia, where Dolley lived as a child

When Dolley was young, most people believed only boys should attend school.

7

Pennsylvania. Dolley liked her new home, but she missed her friends. Her cheerful **personality** made it easy for her to make many new friends.

When Dolley's family moved to Philadelphia, America was still fighting Great Britain in the Revolutionary War (1775–1783). After the war, the United States was a free land. Philadelphia became the capital of the United States. It was a busy city.

In Philadelphia, Dolley met a Quaker lawyer named John Todd, Jr. The couple married in 1790, and two years later, Dolley gave birth to a son, Payne. Another son, William, soon followed.

In the fall of 1793, a terrible **epidemic** of yellow fever broke out in Philadelphia. Yellow fever was a deadly disease spread by mosquito bites. John Todd moved his family out of the city so that they would not catch the disease. After Dolley and her sons were settled in their new home, John returned to Philadelphia to help care for the sick. But he soon became sick with the disease and returned home to be with Dolley and his sons. Sadly, John Todd died shortly after that.

Then Dolley and her baby, William, became sick with yellow fever, too. Dolley recovered from the disease, but little William died. After the epidemic had passed, Dolley and her son, Payne, moved back to Philadelphia.

In the spring of 1794, Philadelphia was once again a busy place. Dolley enjoyed going for walks around the city with Payne. Because she was so attractive, many men noticed her. One of her admirers was James Madison.

Dolley and John Todd lived in this house on Philadelphia's Walnut Street from 1791 to 1793.

JAMES MADISON WAS BORN ON MARCH 16, 1751. HE WAS THE OLDEST child in a large family. James was a smart child, but his health was not good. He suffered from many illnesses.

James lived at Montpelier, his family estate in Orange County, Virginia. His father was a wealthy man who owned a large tobacco **plantation** and many slaves.

James was sent to boarding school when he was 11 years old. Five years later, his father hired a tutor so that all his children could be taught at home.

In 1769, James left home again. This time, he went to the College of New Jersey, now known as Princeton University (right). James was an excellent student. He finished all four years of college in only two years!

While James was in school, he had many friends. He loved having fun and often played jokes on his friends. James and his friends also enjoyed serious discussions. They would talk until late at night about politics. These conversations were the basis for James's future roles in American government.

11

Chapter TWO

A New Husband

When Dolley met James Madison, he was a congressman from Virginia.

JAMES MADISON WAS A CONGRESSMAN FROM Virginia. He was a small man, only 5 feet 6 inches (168 centimeters) tall. He was one of the people who helped to write the United States **Constitution**. Active in the nation's government, James Madison was well respected by many people. And he was very interested in Dolley Payne Todd!

When James Madison met Dolley, he was 42 years old. He was much older than Dolley. She was nervous about meeting the congressman. "The great little Madison has asked to be brought to see me this evening," she wrote to a friend.

James seemed to fall in love with Dolley almost at first sight. Not long after their first meeting, he asked Dolley to be his wife. Dolley was confused and did not know what to do. James was not a Quaker. He went to another church. If she married him, she would no longer be able to attend the Quaker Church.

Dolley was trying to decide what to do about James's marriage proposal when she was asked to meet with Martha Washington—the wife of President George Washington. Dolley had no idea why Mrs. Washington wanted to see her.

Dolley was called to meet with Martha Washington, shown here greeting guests at the White House with her husband.

A drawing of James Madison's family estate, Montpelier

At the meeting, Mrs. Washington asked Dolley, "Are you engaged to James Madison?" Dolley answered, "No, I think not." Mrs. Washington then responded, "Well, if you are, don't be ashamed, be proud. He will make a good husband, all the better for those 17 extra years."

Mrs. Washington also told Dolley that even President Washington hoped she would marry James Madison. Madison had an important career in government ahead of him. He needed someone special to help him.

Mrs. Washington's advice surprised Dolley. She was still confused and did not know what to think. After more thought, however, she agreed to marry James Madison. On September 15, 1794, they were married.

James and Dolley Madison first lived in Philadelphia and then moved to Virginia. They lived on the Madison family estate called Montpelier. Because James was involved in the government, they had many visitors at Montpelier. The Madisons' home became a popular place.

After her marriage to James Madison, Dolley gave up the plain clothes of the Quakers.

Dolley enjoyed having visitors. Her friendly personality made people feel welcome and comfortable at Montpelier. She quickly became a fashionable hostess. She stopped wearing the plain clothes that most Quaker women wore. She began wearing the latest fashions and always looked quite beautiful. James Madison was proud of his new wife.

Thomas Jefferson often came to visit. Jefferson knew James well and respected him. He also enjoyed Montpelier and Dolley's **hospitality**.

In 1801, Jefferson was elected president of the United States. Jefferson asked James to serve as his secretary of state. This was an important job for James Madison, and it led to big changes for both James and Dolley Madison.

Dolley Madison in a portrait from 1804

MONTPELIER WAS THE HOME OF PRESIDENT JAMES MADISON AND his wife, Dolley. Today, this handsome estate is open to the public for tours and special events. Surrounding Montpelier are 2,700 acres (1,094 hectares) of land, formal gardens, and the James Madison Landmark Forest.

Montpelier was settled in 1723. James Madison's grandfather, Ambrose Madison, built the estate. James's father built the original

section of the current home in 1723. James Madison later added two major sections to the house.

After James's death in 1836, Dolley moved back to Washington, D.C. In 1844, she sold Montpelier to a friend. Over the years, the estate was sold five more times. Finally in 1901, the duPont family purchased Montpelier. The duPonts built more additions, doubling the house's size. Members of the duPont family owned Montpelier for more than 80 years.

In 1984, the National Trust for Historic Preservation acquired Montpelier. Five rooms are restored as they would have looked when the Madison family lived there. One room is restored to the era of Marion duPont Scott. The National Trust is planning to open two more duPont rooms and Dolley Madison's bedroom in the near future.

Chapter THREE

Becoming the First Lady

IN 1801, JAMES AND DOLLEY MOVED TO THE
new capital city—Washington, D.C. The city
was still being built, so it was mostly open
fields and swamps. The home of the president
was called the President's Palace. President
Jefferson asked James and Dolley to live in the
palace with him.
They agreed and
soon moved into
the large house.

Thomas
Jefferson's wife
died before he
became president.
At that time, the
first lady was
expected to serve

*A drawing of the new
capital city of
Washington, D.C.*

as hostess at various events. Because he had no wife, Jefferson asked Dolley to serve as hostess on these occasions. So Dolley was the unofficial First Lady during Jefferson's eight years as president. With her experience at Montpelier, Dolley knew how to entertain the important people who came to the President's Palace.

After living with President Jefferson for some time, James and Dolley moved into their own house. But Dolley continued to serve as hostess for Jefferson. She held parties and dances at her own home, too. People throughout Washington, D.C., talked about Dolley Madison's wonderful parties.

Jefferson served two terms as president. In 1808, it was time to elect a new president. James

Thomas Jefferson

During Thomas Jefferson's presidency, Dolley Madison served as hostess at the President's Palace.

▶ In 1812, Dolley
organized the first
wedding at the
White House for
her sister Lucy.

Madison was elected as the fourth president of the United States. It was an exciting time for James and Dolley.

James and Dolley moved back into the President's Palace again. The palace was empty because all the furniture belonged to Jefferson, who removed it when he left. Dolley invited the members of Congress to visit the President's Palace to see the condition of the building. Soon after they visited, they voted to provide money to buy new furnishings for the President's Palace.

As first lady, Dolley brought elegance to Washington, D.C. She became known as a gracious host. She was well known for her Wednesday evening **receptions**. She would invite politicians and the general public to the palace. Her receptions helped to soothe tensions between political parties. She also welcomed visitors from other nations. Foreign visitors were impressed with the events at the President's Palace. Dolley also liked to have parties at the palace for ordinary people. She often gave smaller parties

A plate from the Madison china that Dolley Madison selected as first lady

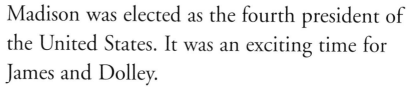

20

and receptions at the palace, too. She also started an egg-rolling event on Easter. Easter-egg hunts are still held each year on the lawn at the White House in Washington, D.C.

Children push hard-boiled eggs at the White House during the annual White House Easter Egg Roll.

James and Dolley Madison enjoyed their four years at the President's Palace. Dolley did a lot to improve the palace when she lived there.

In 1812, it was time for another presidential election. The people liked James Madison as their president and elected him to serve another four years. The next four years for the Madisons would be very different, however.

Chapter FOUR

The Attack on Washington

In 1814, British troops took over Washington, D.C.

DURING JAMES AND DOLLEY MADISON'S FIRST four years in the President's Palace, the United States and Great Britain were not friendly toward each other. The British did not want the United States to sell things to other countries. Finally, in 1812, just before Madison was reelected to office, the conflict exploded into war.

One August day in 1814, during the war, Dolley was getting ready to host a dinner party. James was away with the army. Dolley received an urgent message that the British were in the city of Washington, D.C. They were setting buildings there on fire!

Dolley knew she had to flee from the President's Palace.

Dolley's quick thinking saved many important things from the President's Palace during the British attack.

She was frightened, but she took the time to think. She wanted to save what she could from the President's Palace. She told the servants to pack important papers from the president's office. She had them remove a

Dolley Madison saved this portrait of President George Washington by Gilbert Stuart.

large portrait of George Washington from the wall in the dining room. They quickly packed many other treasures.

Dolley and the treasures from the President's Palace made it to safety. Soon after, the British entered the President's Palace and stole many other valuable items. Then they set the President's Palace on fire. The entire building was in flames.

Luckily, it rained the next morning and the fire was put out before the palace burned to the ground. But the inside was completely ruined, and the outside was badly damaged. Dolley was considered a hero because her quick thinking had saved so many historic items.

The war with Britain finally ended in 1815. The buildings in Washington that had been destroyed by the British were finally rebuilt. While the President's Palace was being rebuilt, James and Dolley had to live in a different

A view of the President's Palace after the British attack

Dolley and James lived in the Octagon House while the President's Palace was being rebuilt.

house called the Octagon House. Dolley missed living in the **mansion**.

After James Madison's term as president ended in 1817, he and Dolley returned to Montpelier. They lived a quiet, happy life there until 1836, when James Madison died. As much as Dolley had enjoyed living at Montpelier, it was now too quiet living there alone without James.

Dolley remembered their life in Washington. She had loved the busy pace of life there, so she decided to move back to Washington.

Many of Dolley's friends, including former presidents, still lived in Washington. She was invited to all the important social events and made many more friends. People could not resist her warm, pleasant personality.

She was such fun to be around. Once again, Dolley was surrounded by people who loved her.

Dolley lived in Washington among her many friends until her death on July 12, 1849. Dolley Madison had been the most important woman in Washington for many years. She was one of the most popular and beloved of all America's first ladies.

This photograph of Dolley Madison was taken in 1848, a year before her death.

IN 1814, AMERICANS WERE proud of the President's Palace. The handsome home of their president was located in their country's capital— Washington, D.C.

At this time in history, America was fighting Britain in the War of 1812. On August 24, 1814, British troops actually **invaded** Washington. They wanted to do something to hurt the pride Americans felt for their capital city. They decided to destroy it. They had spies who discovered which buildings were most important to the country. The British troops there went to each building, destroying them one by one (above).

Although James Madison was not in Washington, Dolley was giving a dinner party that night. When she received warning that the British soldiers were marching toward the palace, she acted immediately. Dolley and the servants worked so quickly that by the time the soldiers arrived, they were gone. The soldiers found the dining room table set for the dinner party. The food was on the table. The soldiers sat down and ate the feast! Then they went through the palace stealing valuables and setting the building on fire.

After the fire at the President's Palace, the remaining walls were blackened by smoke. Soon workers painted them white, and people began to call the President's Palace "the White House." More than 100 years later when Theodore Roosevelt was president, the White House became the building's official name.

1768 Dolley Payne is born on May 20 in North Carolina to Quaker parents John and Mary Coles Payne.

1769 The Payne family moves to a farm in Virginia.

1783 John Payne sells the farm in Virginia, frees the family's slaves, and moves his family to Philadelphia, Pennsylvania.

1790 Dolley marries John Todd, Jr., a Quaker lawyer.

1792 Dolley Payne Todd gives birth to a son, Payne.

1793 Dolley's second son, William, is born. In the fall, an epidemic of yellow fever breaks out in Philadelphia, killing Dolley's husband and their infant son, William.

1794 Dolley Payne Todd meets and marries James Madison.

1801 After her husband becomes secretary of state, Dolley often serves as hostess for President Thomas Jefferson at the President's Palace.

1809 Dolley Madison serves as first lady when her husband becomes the fourth president of the United States.

1814 Dolley Madison saves important papers from the president's office and a portrait of George Washington before British troops burn the President's Palace.

1817 When James Madison's presidential term ends, the couple returns to Montpelier, the Madison family estate in Virginia.

1836 James Madison dies.

1844 Dolley Madison sells Montpelier.

1849 Dolley Payne Todd Madison dies in Washington, D.C.

Glossary TERMS

bonnets (BON-itz)
Bonnets are hats that tie under the chin, worn by babies or women. As a Quaker, Dolley Madison wore gray dresses and plain bonnets.

constitution (kon-stih-TOO-shuhn)
A constitution is a set of basic principles used to govern a state, country, or society. James Madison helped write the U.S. Constitution.

epidemic (ep-ih-DEM-ik)
An epidemic occurs when an infectious disease spreads quickly through a community. Dolley's first husband and second son died during an epidemic of yellow fever.

hospitality (hoss-pih-TAL-ih-tee)
Hospitality is a generous and friendly way of treating guests. Dolley Madison was known for her hospitality.

invaded (in-VAYD-ed)
Invaded means that a place is taken over by armed forces. On August 24, 1814, British troops invaded Washington, D.C.

mansion (MAN-shuhn)
A mansion is a large and fancy house. The President's Palace was a mansion.

personality (pur-suh-NAL-ih-tee)
Personality is all of the special qualities or traits a person has. Dolley Madison had a warm personality.

plantation (plan-TAY-shuhn)
A plantation is a large farm. James Madison's father owned a plantation.

Quakers (KWAY-kurz)
Quakers are Christians who hold simple religious services, wear plain clothes, and oppose war. The Payne family were Quakers.

receptions (ri-SEP-shuhns)
Receptions are formal parties. Dolley Madison gave many receptions at the President's Palace.

For Further INFORMATION

Web Sites

Visit our homepage for lots of links about Dolley Madison:
http://www.childsworld.com/links.html

Note to Parents, Teachers, and Librarians:
We routinely verify our Web links to make sure they're safe,
active sites—so encourage your readers to check them out!

Books

Davidson, Mary R. *Dolley Madison: Famous First Lady.* New York:
Chelsea House, 1992.

Flanagan, Alice K. *Dolley Payne Todd Madison: 1768–1849.* Danbury,
Conn.: Children's Press, 1998.

Patrick, Jean L. S. *Dolley Madison.* Minneapolis, Minn.: Lerner
Publications, 2002.

Pflueger, Lynda. *Dolley Madison: Courageous First Lady.* Springfield,
N.J.: Enslow, 1999.

Places to Visit or Contact

Montpelier
To visit the Madison family estate
11407 Constitution Highway
Montpelier Station, VA 22957
540-672-2728

The James Madison Museum
To see a display of artifacts from the lives of James and Dolley Madison
129 Caroline Street
Orange, VA 22960
540-672-1776

Index